TIME-LIFE
Early Learning Program

The Search
for the
Seven Sisters

TIME
LIFE *for*
Children™

ALEXANDRIA, VIRGINIA

Note to Parents

The Search for the Seven Sisters is designed to introduce young children to the excitement of geography, maps, and world travel. The book invites your child to join Nick, Fran, and their eccentric grandmother as they search for seven look-alike sisters in seven faraway places around the world.

The book contains a number of special features. To give young readers a sense of what it means to travel across vast distances, the journey begins in a small, familiar town and progresses across panoramas of oceans, mountains, plains, forests, and deserts. At each stop along the way, your child will experience the distinctive culture, customs, and language of that country's people. Each destination also offers an interactive searching game that challenges your child to spot the missing sister—as well as a host of other amusing characters and cultural objects.

Finally, an illustrated map at the back of the book encourages your child to retrace the completed journey. To expand on this introduction to geography, mount a simple map of the world on a wall at home. Then use it to talk about countries, continents, and geographical features—or to plan a real or imaginary round-the-world trip with your child.

A Summer Surprise

Hi there! My name is Nick. All year long, my sister Fran and I look forward to our summer vacation. That's when we board the train called the *Padooka Special* and head out to Padooka Falls. What? You've never heard of it? That's where our grandmother lives...

...and here she is now! Her name is Grandma Gumplemeyer, but she likes us to call her Gigi.

This is Gigi's house. It is just like her—warm and full of surprises.

Gigi has a dog named Kumquat.
He is forever getting into trouble.

She also has a swimming pool
shaped like a guitar. That's
where she keeps her pet
trout, Elvis.

There's plenty to do at
Gigi's house.

Sometimes we dance...

...and sometimes we work...

...but we always have fun!

One day we were eating Gigi's world-famous Fudgo-matic-Ultra-Gooey-Banana-Split-Cookie Sundaes when she told us, "This summer we are going to do something completely different. We're going on a search!"

"A search!" we cried out together. "A search for what?"

"A search for my seven sisters," said Gigi, showing us their pictures. "Your great aunts! Each one lives in a distant part of the world. They are very far away."

"They all look just like you!" laughed Fran.

"Yes," agreed Gigi, "they *are* good-looking gals, aren't they? But I haven't seen them in seven years," she added, wiping a tiny tear from her eye. "I miss them very much."

Kate's in the United States.

Dahlia moved to Australia.

Sasha is in Russia.

Natalie's in Italy.

Trina's out in Kenya.

Dinah lives in China.

Coco's gone to Mexico.

Let's go find them!

So we packed and we packed and we packed...

Sasha
in
Russia

Dinah
in China

Pacific
Ocean

Dahlia
in Australia

Natalie in Italy

Kate in the United States

Atlantic Ocean

Coco in Mexico

Trina in Kenya

...until at last we were ready to begin our journey.

Early the next morning, we pedaled out to the Padooka
Falls Airport. Along the way, we waved good-bye to
Ms. Leggett, the fastest mail carrier in the county, and to
Mr. Baigley, the best baker in town.

Ms. Redding, the librarian, leaned from her window and hollered, *"Bon voyage!"*

As Gigi explained, that's French for "Have a good trip!"

Up, Up, and Away!

Traveling in a hot-air balloon, we headed west across the United States. As we floated over the Grand Canyon, we saw people rafting on the Colorado River a mile below.

"They look so tiny from way up here!" said Fran.

"Well," said Gigi, "the Grand Canyon is the largest gorge in the world. It took the Colorado River millions of years to carve it out."

CALIFORNIA

CANADA

TEXAS

MEXICO

12

With a gentle bump, we landed in Wyoming, a state full of cowboys and cowgirls.

To get into the swing of things, we put on all sorts of cowboy clothes: hats, jeans, boots, and chaps. The chaps were made out of leather; they protect your legs from rope burns and cockleburs while you're riding.

Have you seen Kate?

Yup! She's around here somewhere.

Next we visited the reservation of some Indians who have lived in this part of the West for thousands of years. We watched them perform a ceremonial dance.

That night, we camped out under the stars. A singing cowboy named Rex taught us a bunch of cowboy songs. He began to yodel, and a coyote joined in. I think that made Kumquat nervous. Maybe that's why he went to bed early.

In the morning, we met up with a lawman named Sheriff Bill.

"Have you seen my sister Kate 'round these parts?" Gigi asked him.

Why sure! She's at the rodeo. You can't miss her: She's wearing a yellow cowboy hat and a red bandanna!

The rodeo was a true Wild West show! We sat in the bleachers—do you see us? We saw an Indian chief on a dappled horse, and a cowgirl in purple boots. We also found Great Aunt Kate—can you? But we lost Kumquat. Now where can he be?

Can you also find:

- a cowboy wearing yellow spurs
- three rodeo clowns
- a cactus that is not where it should be
- the flag of the United States of America
- Sheriff Bill
- four runaway balloons
- a cowboy wearing a ten-gallon hat
- a bull riding piggyback
- General Custer eating cotton candy
- a covered wagon
- a horse in pajamas
- a drink being spilled on a boy

Kangaroos, Here We Come!

Great Aunt Kate sure could ride that bucking bronco! We spent a week at her home on the range, then hopped a bus headed for California and the Pacific Ocean.

As soon as we got to the Pacific, we set sail for Australia. Along the way we passed the Hawaiian Islands. They have some of the most active volcanoes—and the most incredible surfing— in the world.

"Sit back and enjoy the ride," said Gigi. "The Pacific Ocean is the biggest on Earth, so it will take us many days to reach Australia."

In Australia we set off in a jeep,
searching for Great Aunt Dahlia.
Once we had to stop to let a family
of kangaroos cross the road.

We saw lots of other animals we don't have at home. There was
a furry koala bear, and we even saw a platypus! It
had the bill of a duck, webbed feet, and thick
brown fur.

Then we met a man
named Outback Bob.
He taught us how
to throw a boomerang
so it came right back.

20

G'day, mate!

Outback Bob spoke English, like us, but it was filled with words I had never heard before. If something was good, Bob said it was "bonzer." He called food "tucker," and he called his sheep "jumbucks."

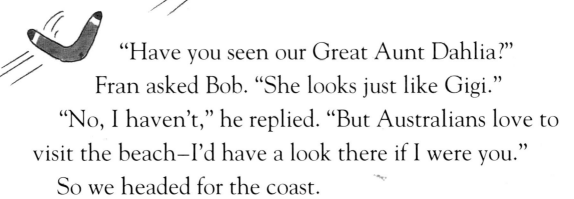

"Have you seen our Great Aunt Dahlia?" Fran asked Bob. "She looks just like Gigi." "No, I haven't," he replied. "But Australians love to visit the beach—I'd have a look there if I were you." So we headed for the coast.

BEACH

We had a "bonzer" time at the beach. Fran and I built a big sandcastle, while Kumquat imitated a kangaroo. Best of all, we found Great Aunt Dahlia! Can you?

Can you also find:

- a boomerang
- a strawberry ice-cream cone
- the flag of Australia
- a three-wheel-drive vehicle
- a scuba diver buying lunch
- an overdressed woman
- four beach books
- a periscope
- a man up to his neck in sand
- three sea stars
- a hungry kangaroo
- a lost skier

ICE CREAM

BEACH GEAR

TUCKER

Checking Out China

Dahlia turned out to be an ace at volleyball! We spent three days playing with her on the beach. Then we said "Good-bye" and boarded a blimp bound for China—and Great Aunt Dinah.

In China, we flew over bright green rice paddies. Gigi pointed out the Great Wall of China, winding away in the distance.

"Wow," said Fran as she snapped a photo. "They weren't kidding when they named this wall 'Great'!"

"You said it!" Gigi replied. "As a matter of fact, the Great Wall of China is the biggest manmade object on Earth. It's the only one that astronauts can see clearly from space."

Quite by accident, we landed in a rice paddy. There we met a farmer named Mr. Wong, who invited us to join his family for lunch.

Mr. Wong's daughter, Lei, showed me how to add and subtract on her abacus.

Mr. Wong's son, Chen-ho, showed Fran how to fly dragon kites. "We Chinese invented kites," Chen-ho proudly said. "And clocks, spaghetti, and fireworks, too!" added Lei.

Mrs. Wong stir-fried meat
and vegetables in a big round
iron skillet called a "wok."

Then she served the food in deep
bowls filled with rice. It was delicious.
And Kumquat was delighted that I was
so clumsy with my chopsticks!

27

After lunch, the Wongs took us to the town market.
"You can find anything at this market," said Mrs. Wong.
"Even our Great Aunt Dinah?" Fran asked.
We all began looking. Gigi saw a man about to trip on a
melon. Kumquat played tag with some ducks. Then we found
Dinah—can you?

Can you also find:
- an abacus
- the flag of China
- a dragon kite
- a big pot of soup
- half a blue bicycle
- a person juggling shoes
- three pairs of chopsticks
- 10 yellow ducks
- a trail of melons
- flying fish

Rushing to Russia

Dinah, who sold toy panda bears in the market, showed us some real panda bears during our stay in China. Then we traveled north to Siberia and climbed aboard a train. We were on our way to find Great Aunt Sasha.

30

Gigi told us that our train, the Trans-Siberian Railroad, would take seven days to reach Moscow, the capital of Russia.

Outside it was summer. Herds of reindeer grazed on plains covered in green. For most of the year, however, Siberia lies buried deep in snow. A Siberian woman showed us a picture of her house in winter. How would you like to shovel *that* walkway?

A week later we arrived in Moscow. We headed straight for Red Square–that's the heart of the city–but Great Aunt Sasha was nowhere to be seen.

We came across some gymnasts giving an exhibition.
"Many of the world's best gymnasts are Russian," said Gigi.
A girl named Tatyana did a fantastic flip on the balance beam.
"I hope to be in the Olympics some day!"
she announced.

Tatyana took us to meet her brother, Ivan, at his ballet school. When he grows up, Ivan wants to dance in the Bolshoi Ballet. I think Kumquat may become a great dancer, too.

"Let's look for Sasha at the Moscow Circus," Gigi suggested. "She always did enjoy a spectacle."

"Tickets, please!" said the clown at the circus gate.

"Why don't I recognize all those letters?" asked Fran.

"Because we use a different alphabet," replied the clown. "That sign says 'Circus' in Russian."

And what a splendid circus it was! The famous Russian bears rode about on motorbikes, while the trained seals honked up a storm. Even Kumquat got into the act!

To top it all off, we found Great Aunt Sasha—can you?

Can you also find:

- a spectator with a trunk
- twin tigers
- a musical banana
- a man on stilts
- a snake serving sodas
- a bird on a boy
- a heap of hula hoops
- an airborne acrobat
- a bear who joined the band
- a low-wire act

Giddily to Italy

Great Aunt Sasha had joined the circus as a juggler! After the show, Sasha's friend Alexei, a stunt pilot, offered to fly us to Italy.

On our way to Italy, we flew over the
Alps. They are huge, rugged, snow-capped
mountains. Alexei couldn't resist doing loop-
the-loops and barrel rolls. Kumquat just loved it!

At the airport in Italy, we met a cab driver named Carlo. We asked him to take us to Venice, where Great Aunt Natalie lives. Instead, Carlo drove us to Pisa!

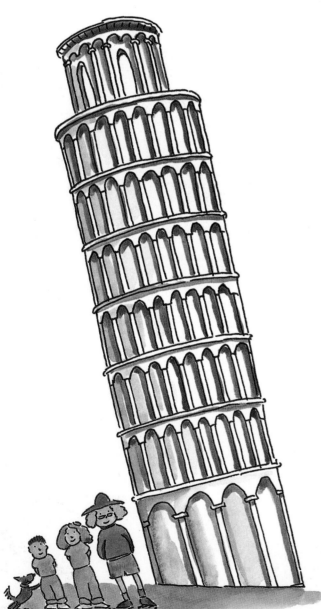

"Are you sure this is the way to Venice?" asked Gigi.

"It's just a little detour I dreamed up!" said Carlo. "You can't visit Italy without seeing the Leaning Tower of Pisa! Say 'cheese' and I'll take your picture. *Perfetto!* You look so nice!"

Next Carlo drove us to a pasta shop in Rome. I never knew spaghetti came in so many shapes and colors!

Some green fettucine and some orange tortellini, please!

"And now," said Carlo, "for a game of football—or, as you Americans call it, 'soccer.'"

We sat in the stands and ate scrumptious Italian ice cream called *gelato*.

When the game ended, Carlo took us to Venice, the city with canals for streets. We were sad to say good-bye, but Carlo cheered us up with some advice: "Your Great Aunt Natalie would love the Grand Canal! Why don't you look for her there?"

So we sat in a café beside the Grand Canal and watched the gondolas drifting by. Carlo was right! We soon spotted Great Aunt Natalie. Have you?

Can you also find:
- two soggy hats
- a lost submarine
- a lion with wings
- two flags of Italy
- six tourists taking pictures
- a fresh fish dinner
- two soccer balls
- 13 striped poles
- a wading waiter
- a sailor stretching his legs

An African Adventure

Natalie turned out to be a gondolier. She rowed us through all the canals of Venice.

Then Gigi said, "Let's go find Trina in Kenya!" So we sailed south, across the Mediterranean Sea, until we landed in Egypt. That's a country in Africa.

Near the Great Pyramids, we hitched a ride with a caravan of camels. They were about to cross the Sahara Desert.

"This is the biggest desert in the world," said Gigi.

It felt like the hottest, too! We had to wear special clothes to protect us from the sun.

As we traveled toward Kenya, we met people from many different East African tribes. They waved to us and called out, "Jambo!" That means "Hello!" in Swahili.

In Kenya, we stayed in a farming village. Its houses were round and made of mud, with roofs of grass.

I made friends with a boy named Jomo and helped him carry water from the river to his house. Balancing a big pot of water on your head is a lot harder than it looks!

The next morning, we visited a Masai tribe. A girl named Kahla gave Fran and Gigi some beautiful necklaces made from colored glass beads.

That night, we watched the elders perform a Masai dance. They wore paint on their legs and faces, and danced with spears and shields.

Next we traveled to snowy Mount Kilimanjaro. At the base of the mountain was Tsavo National Park.

"This is where Trina works!" cried Gigi. "Let's see if we can find her!"

45

"Is this a zoo?" Fran asked when we entered the park.

"No," said Gigi. "It's a wildlife preserve, a place where animals are protected from hunters."

We saw enough different creatures to fill Noah's Ark many times over! And lucky us—we found Great Aunt Trina! Can you?

Can you also find:

- an elephant who is squirting and being squirted
- two hippos showing off their teeth
- the flag of Kenya
- a tree full of lions
- a flying flamingo
- two swinging apes
- a checkered zebra
- four loping antelopes
- a lion with a sweet tooth
- two cheetahs giving chase
- a snake in a tree
- a rhinoceros about to jump out of its skin

Cruising to Mexico

Trina was a park ranger. Together we hiked up Mount Kilimanjaro, where we had a magnificent view of the park below. But soon it was time to leave.

"One more sister to go!" said Gigi. "Mexico, here we come!"

From Kenya we sailed south to the Cape of Good Hope, at the tip of Africa. A school of whales led us into the Atlantic Ocean.

"Those whales migrate thousands of miles a year," said Gigi.

"I'm sure we've traveled that far, too!" said Fran.

Weeks later, we arrived on the coast of Mexico and took a train to Mexico City. Gigi told me that 19 million people live here! Then she said, "If I know Coco, we'll find her at the fiesta!"

Like the city, the fiesta was crowded. While Kumquat did a Mexican hat dance, we ate fresh tortillas and watched some kids trying to break open a *piñata*–that's a paper donkey filled with candy. Finally, we found Great Aunt Coco. I bet you can, too!

Can you also find:
- a bull who has switched places with a matador
- a donkey taking a siesta
- an eagle biting a snake
- a game of hide-and-seek
- a woman with a tray of pastries on her head
- an Aztec dancer
- the flag of Mexico
- a bird sneaking off with a snack

Coco played the maracas in a mariachi band! She took us all over Mexico, then put us on a plane for home.

By the time we got back to Padooka Falls, everyone was dog-tired—especially Kumquat!

On a map, we drew our route around the world. Can you follow it with your finger?

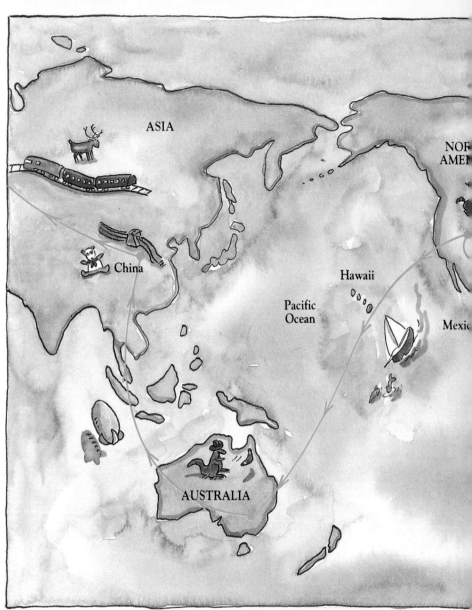

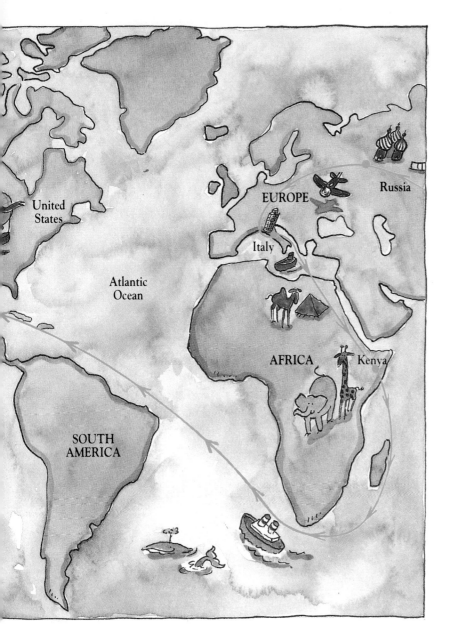

Then Gigi said, "That was a terrific trip, but I miss my sisters already! I won't see them again for a very long time."

Kumquat, why are you scratching at the door?

It was Kate, Dahlia, Dinah, Sasha, Natalie, Trina, and Coco!

The search for the seven sisters was over.
But the seven-year reunion had just begun!

Isn't the world a wonderful place?

TIME-LIFE for CHILDREN™
Publisher: Robert H. Smith
Managing Editor: Neil Kagan
Editorial Directors: Jean Burke Crawford,
    Patricia Daniels, Allan Fallow,
    Karin Kinney, Sara Mark
Editorial Coordinator: Elizabeth Ward
Director of Marketing: Margaret Mooney
Product Manager: Cassandra Ford
Assistant Product Manager: Shelley L. Schimkus
Production Manager: Prudence G. Harris
Administrative Assistant: Rebecca C. Christoffersen
Special Contributor: Jacqueline A. Ball

Produced by Joshua Morris Publishing, Inc.
Wilton, Connecticut 06897.
Series Director: Michael J. Morris
Creative Director: William N. Derraugh
Illustrator: Chris Demarest
Author: Michael Chesworth
Designers: Michael Chesworth, Brien O'Reilly

CONSULTANTS
Dr. Lewis P. Lipsitt, an internationally recognized specialist on childhood development, was the 1990 recipient of the Nicholas Hobbs Award for science in the service of children. He serves as science director for the American Psychological Association and is a professor of psychology and medical science at Brown University, where he is director of the Child Study Center.
Dr. Judith A. Schickedanz, an authority on the education of preschool children, is an associate professor of early childhood education at the Boston University School of Education, where she also directs the Early Childhood Learning Laboratory. Her published work includes *More Than the ABC's: Early Stages of Reading and Writing Development* as well as several textbooks and many scholarly papers.

First printing. Printed in Hong Kong.
Published simultaneously in Canada.

Time Life Inc. is a wholly owned subsidiary of THE TIME INC. BOOK COMPANY.

TIME-LIFE is a trademark of Time Warner Inc. U.S.A.

Time Life Inc. offers a wide range of fine publications, including home video products. For subscription information, call 1-800-621-7026, or write TIME-LIFE BOOKS, P.O. Box C-32068, Richmond, Virginia 23261-2068.

Library of Congress Cataloging in Publication Data
The Search for the seven sisters : a hidden-picture geography book / the editors of Time-Life, Inc.

      p. cm.–(Time-Life early learning program)
    Summary: Grandmother Gigi, her grandchildren, and her dog travel around the world in search of her seven sisters, each of whom must be found among the illustrations of a particular country's clothing, food, sports, and other cultural facets.

    ISBN 0-8094-9287-3 (trade).—ISBN 0-8094-9288-1 (lib. bdg.)

    [1. Geography—Fiction. 2. Voyages around the world—Fiction. 3. Grandmothers—Fiction. 4. Picture puzzles.] I. Time-Life for Children (Firm) II. Series.
PZ7.S4393   1991
[E]—dc20
                           91-32892
                               CIP
                               AC